Bertram Lang

Aus der Reihe: e-fellows.net stipendiaten-wissen

e-fellows.net (Hrsg.)

Band 675

A Book Review of Rey-Ching Lu (2011) "Chinese Democracy and Elite Thinking"

Der GRIN Verlag publiziert seit 1998 wissenschaftliche Arbeiten von Studenten, Hochschullehrern und anderen Akademikern als eBook und gedrucktes Buch. Die Verlagswebsite www.grin.com ist die ideale Plattform zur Veröffentlichung von Hausarbeiten, Abschlussarbeiten, wissenschaftlichen Aufsätzen, Dissertationen und Fachbüchern.

Document Nr. V211217

Bertram Lang

Aus der Reihe: e-fellows.net stipendiaten-wissen

e-fellows.net (Hrsg.)

Band 675

A Book Review of Rey-Ching Lu (2011) "Chinese Democracy and Elite Thinking"

GRIN Verlag

Die Deutsche Bibliothek verzeichnet diese Publikation in der Deutschen Nationalbibliografie; detaillierte bibliografische Daten sind im Internet über http://dnb.d-nb.de/ abrufbar.

1. Auflage 2012
Copyright © 2012 GRIN Verlag GmbH
http://www.grin.com
Druck und Bindung: Books on Demand GmbH, Norderstedt Germany
ISBN 978-3-656-39336-8

Albert-Ludwigs-Universität Freiburg (Germany) 18 February 2012
Seminar Democracy & Development:
A Comparative Asian Perspective

Book review of: *Rey-Ching Lu (2011): Chinese*
Democracy and Elite Thinking.

Author: Bertram Lang

Outline:

1.   Introduction

> China has favorable prospects for becoming a multiparty democracy; any democratic system that emerges likely will be a Confucian democracy (communal or social democracy) (Lu 2011: Preface, X).

The question whether China will or will not follow a path of democratic reforms in the near future has been repeatedly asked by many scholars over the last years, even decades. Pessimists usually tend to argue that despite considerable economic reforms, the Chinese Communist Party's (CCP) political grasp over Chinese mainland society is growing ever tighter and stronger. (see Pei 2008, Shambaugh 2008).

Among the notorious optimists, Henry Rowen stands out for his – albeit premature – forecast of a political opening and democratic transition of Chinese society as a natural consequence of its economic liberalization and fast-growing prosperity (cf. Rowen 1996). But after decades of contradictory results of quantitative studies on the alleged causal relationship between economic development and democracy, deterministic perspectives should be judged with a very critical eye and many scholars today rather agree with Lipset's statement that "[w]hether democracy succeeds or fails continues to depend significantly on the choices, behaviors, and decisions of political leaders and groups" (Lipset 1994: 18).

Thus, Rey-Ching Lu's recently published book "Chinese democracy and elite thinking" is completely in line with what the German political scientist Wolfgang Muno describes as the "need for qualitative analyses of [...] important actors, concepts and strategies, as well through case studies as through the comparison of few cases" (Muno 2001: 50)[1]. Instead of looking at economic or social data on the Chinese society as a whole, Lu chooses to focus upon the ideas and convictions of a few members of the mainland's elite, from which he draws conclusions about China's political development in the next couple of years. The underlying assumption is that, contrary to many Western theorists' beliefs, it is neither the middle class nor the economic liberalisation in itself that will spark democracy 'from the bottom', but rather the changing attitudes of the more and more globalised social elite that will eventually lead to a top-down process of political reform and liberalisation.

This short review focuses on the most important aspects of Lu's methodological approach and line of argument. After a presentation of his methodological proceeding, the main findings and conclusions of Lu's study will be described and discussed. Then, a critical assessment of the author's arguments will be made, also considering other scholars' views on the issues of China's possible democratization and the role of its elites in this process.

---

[1] „Notwendig sind qualitative Analysen von [...] wichtigen Akteuren, Konzepten und Strategien, sowohl im Einzelfall wie beim Vergleich weniger Fälle."

2.   Methodological considerations

In order to assess China's democratic development and to draw conclusions about its future, Rey-Ching Lu opts for a two-pronged methodological approach. In a first step, he resorts to a historiographical analysis of China's history since the beginning of what Chinese refer to as the *quru* (humiliation) period in 1839[2], with the aim of proving the causal relationship between the "development and change of Chinese society" and "Chinese historical practice of democracy"(Lu 2011: 20). Secondly, so as to extrapolate these historical trends of Chinese society toward the next 20 years, Lu conducts 120 interviews with members of the Chinese elite, subdivided into four groups: government officials, businesspeople, media professionals and intellectuals (cf. ibid.: 21). This choice is justified with reference to the traditionally crucial role of Chinese elites in leading and educating the masses (cf. ibid.: 4) and with the assertion that significant changes in Chinese society can only be understood or foreseen through the analysis of "China's subtle political language" (ibid.: 10) and its particular, collectivist culture:

> In Chinese culture, an individual does not see himself as an independent, self-seeking entity with a subjectivity that cannot be penetrated by any collectivity; instead, each individual sees himself as a part of various social relationships that he enjoys being a part of and is ready and willing to make contribution by devoting himself to the collective good (Lu 2011: 7).

However, from the 120 interviews conducted the author chooses to take only 18 interview cases from Shanghai into account for the present study. Lu's justification for substantially limiting the sample is that Shanghai is the most westernized of the big cities in China and that therefore "Shanghai could best represent the future of China as a fusion of Chinese culture and Western culture" (Lu 2011: 23). Yet, Lu doesn't want Shanghai to be understood as being representative of China as a whole. Unfortunately, as the author chooses not to present any information about the other 102 interviews, any comparison between the Shanghai interviews and the overwhelmingly larger remaining part of the covered data is impossible.

3.   Findings and prognoses

The first and foremost result of Lu's study is the one quoted at the very beginning: That China will indeed follow a path of democratization within the observed period, that is to say until 2024, thanks to a cultural blend of modern Western (i.e., liberal, democratic, individualist) and traditional Chinese (i.e. Confucian, collectivist) norms. But Lu is even more audacious in his prognosis: From the attitudes expressed by the 18 aforementioned interviewees in Shanghai, he concludes

---

[2] The First Opium War, which started in 1839 and ended in 1842 with the first of the so-called *unequal treaties*, the Treaty of Nanjing, is generally considered to be the starting point of China's forced and troublesome modernisation process.

that this process of democratization will start with the intellectual elite and then spread over the whole society (cf. Lu 2011: 143). Finally, as implied by his case selection, Lu also suggests that these developments will be sparked off in Shanghai before spreading to the rest of China. In order to shed light on the foundations of these strong theses, the thrust of Lu's line of argument will be presented in the following paragraphs, dealing separately with the historical analysis (Chapters 2 to 5) and the presentation of the interview cases (Chapters 6 to 8).

The first, historiographical part of the book is subdivided into four periods of modern Chinese history: The waning Qing Dynasty (1839-1911), the Republican era (1911-49), Mao Zedong's rule (1949-76) and the Reform era (since 1978). According to Lu's general theoretical assumptions, each period is approached from the angle of developments and controversies within the intellectual elite, supposing that "the Chinese intellectual elite, the educated stratum, has been both the political and/or cultural leaders of the society and the driving force of societal change" (Lu 2011: 29). Thus, the late Qing era is described as a period of extreme confusion and dismay among Chinese intellectuals, being confronted with the unpromising task of saving China from both Western and Japanese aggressive superiority (cf. ibid.:30). Most importantly, after the complete failure of the (militaristic) Self-strengthening Movement, the "Hundred Days Reform", initiated in 1898 by progressive thinkers like Liang Qichao, brought upon the first political opening towards a constitutional monarchy, before falling victim to the forced restoration under Ci Xi (cf. ibid.: 31-33). After the failure of the reformist approach, the following revolutionary approach led by Sun Yat-Sen is presented by Lu as the first "integration of Confucian doctrine and Western thoughts" (ibid.: 35). Thus, the early Republican era with its parliamentary democracy appears as an important reference point for Lu's normative conception of a Chinese-style democratic system. Consequentially, Lu's interest in the ensuing Warlord period from 1916 to 1928 lies with a new intellectual Enlightenment movement in Beijing which blended Western individualist ideas with a nationalist devotion to the country's destiny (cf. ibid.: 38). Its protagonist, Hu Shi, is later presented as "a very good example of a patriotic intellectual driven by nationalism" who, at the same time, "advocated liberalism and individualism" (ibid.: 131).

As to Mao's rule, Lu states that notwithstanding the officially Marxist-Leninist rhetoric, Mao remained in large parts what he was at the beginning: a Confucian intellectual. This eccentric interpretation is mainly substantiated by the ideal of "selfless sacrifice for the sake of all" (ibid.: 50) supposedly inherent in both ideologies. According to Lu, Mao's grave failure was to opt for the idea of ongoing revolution instead of the Confucian path of limited revolution leading to harmony (cf. ibid.). The core of Mao's inhumane system was therefore rooted in the artificial division of the

whole society into the people and its enemies (cf. ibid.: 57-59). Lu opposes this discriminatory model to the meritocratic ideal of a 'true' Confucian system in which "[e]verybody was born equal and had the same capability and opportunity to become a saint" (Lu 2011: 60). The idealized picture of Confucian teaching which shines through these lines is quite remarkable.

Surprisingly, none of the presented periods is as harshly disparaged by Lu as the Reform period since 1978. Not only have the economic reforms served the sole purpose of rebuilding the Communist party's legitimacy, but the insistence on political dictatorship and the abuse of political power for economic purposes have led to the emergence of a very powerful elite group of rent-seeking bureaucrats and corrupt businessmen. Capitalist values provided the "justification of the predatory coalition of the elite" (ibid.: 70), at the expense of the lower classes in an ever more un-equal society. All this culminates in the ostentatious rediscovery of Confucian ideals by the ruling classes over the last years, which is by no means welcomed by the author: "Therefore, once again, Confucianism becomes the tool of dictatorial governance for the ruler - a constant tragedy that happened repeatedly in Chinese history" (ibid.). Thus, Lu accuses the political leaders of abandon-ing the Confucian ideal of governing in the interest of the whole people in order to preserve the in-terests of the party alone (cf. ibid.: 61-70).

In the second, empirical part, the author starts by giving an account of every individual inter-view, with particular attention being paid to the interviewees' self-view, their attitude towards Shanghai's development, the government's role in it and their hopes for the future generation.[3] The ensuing conclusions about the respective attitudes of the aforementioned elite groups can be summarized as follows[4]: Party cadres still hold idealized views of their own and the CCP's role of serving the collective interest of the people. Their traditional, nationalist value system leaves no room for democratic ideals. However, potential for change could be seen in a younger, more indi-vidualist generation of party officials. (cf. ibid.: 80; 132). While the enterprise people have mostly managed to combine traditional and modern values in their own lives and may therefore be able to act as "pioneers of the global culture" (ibid.: 90) in China, they are too convinced of the positive role of government in economic development to support demands for substantial political change. Surprisingly, the media professionals express overwhelmingly negative views on the govern-ment's restrictive role. Even without evoking explicit democratic ideals, most of them wish to su-pervise the government more independently (ibid.: 95; 105-108). As for the intellectuals, Lu

---

[3] Lu chooses not to ask directly about attitudes toward democracy, but to derive his conclusions from the general attitudes expressed by the interviewees on the mentioned issues.
[4] There is further cause for criticism regarding the selection of the interviewees. For instance, the interviewed businesspeople are essentially working for multinational companies or have a Taiwanese background themselves. Media people are exclusively newspaper journalists, whereas the selection of intellectuals shows a clear bias toward history and philosophy professors.

stresses that they "all carried a spirit of social responsibility, and all were concerned about the fate of the nation" (ibid.: 128). While disagreeing on concrete reform measures and ways to handle sensitive issues like the Taiwan problem, they all see (some form of) democracy as the future of China and underline the importance of independent scholarship to achieve it (cf. Lu 2011: 128). Lu therefore concludes that both intellectuals' and most media professionals' views support his hypothesis of a fusion of nationalism and democratic ideals within the Chinese elite, because "their nationalism made them see that democratic ideals would benefit this nation" (ibid.: 141).

4.   Critical assessment

With regard to Lu's historical analysis, it is astonishing to see the quite romantic picture he draws of traditional Chinese society. For instance, the non-emergence of a Western-style political system based on "fairness of open power competition and majority rule" (Lu 2011: 2) is explained solely by the supposed "harmony between the ruling elite and the ruled citizens" (ibid.), which in turn can be traced back to the ideas of Confucian teaching which "see the emperor-subject relationship as that of father-son" (ibid.). Even without contesting the important role of Confucian ethics in legitimizing the traditional Chinese system, the conclusions Lu derives from his historical analysis concerning the "role of elites in leading and educating the mass peasants to live a moral life that complies with the natural law of the universe" (ibid.: 3) appear somewhat questionable. Especially the notion of the Confucian elite as a "driving force of societal change" (ibid.: 29) is a very daring one, considering the extreme conservatism of the Chinese upper class over the last decades or even centuries of imperial rule.

Obviously, the rigid distinction between Asian values (esp. Chinese collectivism and nationalism) on the one hand and Western values (liberalism and democracy) on the other, as well as the emphasis on the outstanding role of the elites in reconciling those two categories, serve as justification for both the author's theoretical assumptions and methodological approach. However, the attribution of *democracy* as a Western value is highly contestable and has been most famously disproved by Amartya Sen, referring to the "long history of public reasoning across the world" (Sen 2006a; see also Sen 2006b). In Lu's defence, it has to be said that this reproach holds even more for many Western scholars, whereas Lu himself develops a distinctive Chinese model of democracy, declaring Confucianism to be compatible with basic democratic values (cf. Lu 2011: 60). Other scholars like Michael Collins have even asserted that forms of democratic participation are not merely possible, but rather a *sine qua non* of true self-fulfilment in Confucian ethics (cf. Collins 2008: 161; 171 et seq.).

Having said that, Lu's (normative and predictive) model of "Confucian democracy" is as well susceptible to some criticism for being rather vague and – at least in its occurrence as a predictive model – strongly idealized. In fact, the latter is a general problem with Lu's argumentation, which in most parts fails to draw a clear-cut distinction between normative (*Which model would be good for China in the future?*) and predictive (*In which direction way will the country actually develop?*) aspects. As to the blurry definition of "Confucian democracy", it is repeatedly described as implying a "social democracy or communal democracy, with the Great Harmony its spiritual, ethical, and cultural contents" (Lu 2011: 60). This problem may be partly mitigated by the concept of "deep democracy" introduced at the very end of the book, which in Lu's view is "consistent with Confucian political ideal ("Great Harmony") and the ideal of political liberalism" (ibid.: 148). This concept mainly refers to economic justice, political participation of different groups in society and the building of social capabilities independent from social, cultural and ethical backgrounds:

> Deep democracy and the social capability approach, with its nature of completeness, do address these problems *both* in the immediate need of overcoming corruption and seriously unjust social division *and* in the long-term need of overcoming political dictatorship (Lu 2011: 148, emphasis by author).

But even if we accept Lu's generalizations regarding the different elite groups' general attitudes, even if we assume that intellectuals are primarily committed to the people's well-being or that party-cadres believe in their self-commitment for the collective interest, it is hard to see why politics in China should suddenly swerve from what Lu denounces as a "predatory economy" (ibid.: 62) with purely rent-seeking elites towards a social democracy committed to the interests of the poor and the powerless. With reference to the interviewed party officials, Lu describes a generational swift from an old (i.e. collectivist) value system towards much more individualistic, self-centered values in the younger generation (cf. ibid.: 133). Yet, there is a strong ambiguity in Lu's conception of 'individualism': On the one hand, he uses it synonymously with "Western" and "democratic" values, on the other hand, it has a very negative connotation when applied to the businesspeople or the middle-class[5] who are both accused of a self-centered attitude, caring only for their own (material) well-being instead of looking at the interests of all (cf. Lu 2011: 62-68).

There is some ground for more general scepticism vis-à-vis Lu's optimistic prognoses as well. Minxin Pei has warned against the temptation to confound economic reforms and modernization with a reduction of the CCP's will to cling on to political power:

> There is a critical distinction between liberalization and democratization. Evidence of the former is fairly abundant. Plainly, economic progress and social change are making for a more diverse, plura-

---

[5] Lu here refers to He, Qinglian (2007) who, in his paper "The New Myth in China: China's Rising Middle-Class Will Accelerate Democratization" argues that this will precisely not be the case because the middle class are the main beneficiaries of the current political and economic order (cf. Lu 2011: 66).

listic, and assertive society. […] Yet in spite of all this, there are as yet no real institutional channels through which societal interests, political groups, and ordinary citizens can influence the selection of rulers or the making of public policy (Pei 2007: 56).

While Dali L. Yang agrees with Lu on the issue of a possible adaptation of the Chinese elite to democratic norms, which he thinks may occur thanks to China's further integration in an international system governed by democratic ideals (cf. Yang 2007: 62), he also underscores the important role of other forces in society: "Ultimately, China's political transformation will not be determined by the top elite alone, but will be subject to negotiation and contestation among diverse interests in state and society" (ibid.).

5.   Conclusion

Rey-Ching Lu's book has the merit of putting forward a clear and provocative statement, which, instead of merely looking at overall statistical indicators, is grounded in the author's deep insight into Chinese society in the past and present. Having said that, it has become evident that "Chinese Democracy and Elite Thinking" is also prone to substantial criticism, both regarding its methodology and its hypotheses.

   After all, it is hard to imagine that a substantial institutional change towards democracy in China should be brought about solely by an internal shift in elite thinking. As Heike Holbig has pointed out, the ideological framework of the CCP's rule is not only substantial for its claim to represent the interest of the 'common people' (cf. Holbig 2009: 31-32), but also imposes significant restrictions on the possibilities of institutional change. The question of a possible democratic shift (initiated in a "top-down" manner by the social elites) therefore substantially remains one of political stability and regime legitimacy. Without a significant and critical challenge external to the new and old elite circles, it is hard to see why those elites should be driven to a redefinition of ideology towards the effective inclusion of democratic norms, which in itself poses the risk of delegitimizing the current system. Thus, only such a systemically dangerous external challenge to authoritarianism and one-party-rule may eventually force the CCP to include more liberal norms into its ideological framework.

References

Collins, Michael (2008): China's Confucius and Western Democracy. In: *Contemporary Review*, Vol. 290/1689, pp. 161-172.

He, Qinglian (2007): *The New Myth in China: China's Rising Middle-Class Will Accelerate Democratization*. URL: http://www.360doc.com/content/07/0731/10/21426_644689.shtml (2012/01/30).

Heberer, Thomas; Schubert, Gunter (ed.) (2009): *Regime legitimacy in contemporary China. Institutional change and stability*. London; New York: Routledge.

Holbig, Heike (2009): Ideological reform and political legitimacy in China. Challenges in the post-Jian era. In: Thomas Heberer and Gunter Schubert (ed.): *Regime Legitimacy in Contemporary China. Institutional Change and Stability*. London; New York: Routledge, pp. 13–34.

Lipset, Seymour Martin (1994): The Social Requisites of Democracy Revisited. In: *American Sociological Review*, Vol. 59, No. 1 (Feb. 1994), pp. 1-22.

Lu, Rey-Ching (2011): *Chinese Democracy and Elite Thinking*. New York: Palgrave Macmillan.

Muno, Wolfgang (2001): *Demokratie und Entwicklung* [Democracy and Development]. Mainz: Inst. für Politikwiss., Abt. Politische Auslandsstudien und Entwicklungspolitik.

Pei, Minxin (2007): How Will China Democratize? In: *Journal of Democracy*, Vol. 18/3, July 2007, pp. 53-57.

Pei, Minxin (2008): *China's Trapped Transition: The Limits of Developmental Autocracy*. 1st Harvard Paperback ed. Cambridge, MA; London: Harvard University Press.

Rowen, Henry S. (1996): The Short March: China's Road to Democracy. In: *National Interest*, Vol. 45, pp. 61–70.

Sen, Amartya (2006a): Democracy Isn't 'Western'. In: *Wall Street Journal*, 24 March 2006, p. A10. URL: http://arthshastra.com/pdf/DemocracyIsntWestern.pdf (2012/01/30).

Sen, Amartya (2006b): *Identity and Violence. The Illusion of Destiny*. New York: Norton.

Shambaugh, David (2008): China's Communist Party: Atrophy and Adaptation. Washington, DC: Woodrow Wilson Center Press.

Yang, Dali L. (2007): China's Long March to Freedom. In: *Journal of Democracy*, Vol. 18/3, July 2007, pp. 58-64.